COBOL Programming Interview Questions, Answers and Explanations

By Terry Sanchez-Clark

ITCOOKBOOK

COBOL Programming Interview Questions and Answers Book
1-933804-45-9

Compiled by Terry Sanchez-Clark
ITCOOKBOOK

Edited by Emilee Newman Bowles

The programs in this book have been included for instructional value only. They have been tested with care but are not guaranteed for any particular purpose. The publisher does not offer any warranties or representations not does it accept any liabilities with respect to the programs.

Trademarks: All trademarks are the property of their respective owners. Equity Press is not associated with any product or vender mentioned in this book.

Please visit our website at www.itcookbook.com

Table of Contents

5

Introduction

Many people might question the need - at this late date of 2007 - for an interview questions book on the COBOL programming language. That is to say, many people would wonder if there are any jobs out there for COBOL programmers. Practitioners know, however, that there is a vibrant job market for these skills. As more of the baby-boomer generation retire from active employment, who will fill these much needed positions? Smart programmers who want to make a good living at their trade.

This book published with you, the Information Technology job seeker in mind – the contractor or employee who knows that all you need is a few good books to get the learning started, and eventually, the job done. So here is the COBOL Interview Questions guide. I hope it will show you what you need to know, and what you can safely ignore. This book will help guide your learning and help you land your next COBOL programming assignment. Good Luck!

Jim Stewart
Publisher
Equity Press

Question 01: Sections in Data Division

How many sections are there in Data Division?

A: It has six sections:

1. FILE SECTION
2. WORKING-STORAGE SECTION
3. LOCAL-STORAGE SECTION
4. SCREEN SECTION
5. REPORT SECTION
6. LINKAGE SECTION

In COBOL II, there are only 4 sections:

1. FILE SECTION
2. WORKING-STORAGE SECTION
3. LOCAL-STORAGE SECTION
4. LINKAGE SECTION

Question 02: Dynamic or a Static Module

How can I tell if a module is being called dynamically or statically?

A: The only way is to look at the output of the linkage editor (IEWL) or the load module itself. If the module is being called DYNAMICALLY, then it will not exist in the main module. If it is being called STATICALLY, then it will be seen in the load module. Calling a working storage variable, containing a program name, does not make a DYNAMIC call. This type of calling is known as IMPLICITE calling as the name of the module is implied by the contents of the working storage variable. Calling a program name literal (CALL).

Question 03: Advantages of VS COBOL II Over OS/VS COBOL

What are the advantages of VS COBOL II over OS/VS COBOL?

A: The working storage and linkage section limit has been increased. They have 128 megabytes as supposed to 1 megabyte in OS/VS COBOL. In using COBOL on PC we have only flat files and the programs can access only limited storage. Whereas in VS COBOL II on M/F, the programs can access up to 16MB or 2GB depending on the addressing and can use VSAM files to make I/O operations faster.

Question 04: Steps in Creating a COBOL Program

What are the steps in creating a COBOL program executable?

A: DB2 pre-compiler (if embedded SQL is used), CICS translator (if CICS program), COBOL compiler, Link editor. If DB2 program, create plan by binding the DBRMs.

Question 05: Compiling a Program without Errors

What are the minimum requirements to compile a program without errors?

Is compute w=u a valid statement?

When will you prefer compute statement over the move statement in the above example?

A: Look into the Identification Division. Go to > Program-ID > Program-name.

Compute w=u is a valid statement. It is equivalent to move u to w.

When significant left-order digits would be lost in execution, the COMPUTE statement can detect the condition and allow you to handle it. The MOVE statement carries out the assignment with destructive truncation. Therefore, if the size error needs to be detected, COMPUTE will be preferred over MOVE. The ON SIZE ERROR phrase of COMPUTE statement, compiler generates code to detect size-overflow.

Question 06: Difference between Dynamic and Static in COBOL

What is the difference between a DYNAMIC and STATIC call in COBOL?

A: All called modules cannot run standalone if they require program variables passed to them via the LINKAGE section. Dynamically called modules are those that are not bound with the calling program at link edit time (IEWL for IBM) and so are loaded from the program library (joblib or steplib) associated with the job. For dynamic calling of a module the DYNAM compiler option must be chosen. Else the linkage editor will not generate an executable as it will expect null address resolution of all called modules.

A statically called module is one that is bound with the calling module at link edit, and therefore becomes part of the executable load module.

Question 07: Associating Files with External Data Sets

How will you associate your files with external data sets where they physically reside?

A: Using SELECT clause, the files can be associated with external data sets. The SELECT clause is defined in the FILE-CONTROL paragraph of Input-Output Section that is coded Environment Division. The File structure is defined by FD entry under File-Section of Data Division for the OS.

Question 08: Definition of File in Operating System

How will you define your file to the operating system?

A: Associate the file with the external data set using SELECT clause of INPUT-OUTPUT SECTION WHICH.

INPUT-OUTPUT SECTION appears inside the ENVIRONMENT DIVISION.

Define your file structure in the FILE SECTION of DATA DIVISION.

Question 09: Use of Declaratives in COBOL

What are the uses of Declaratives in COBOL?

A: Declaratives provide special sections that are executed when an exceptional condition occurs. They must be grouped together and coded at the beginning of procedure division, and the entire procedure division must be divided into sections.

The Declaratives start with a USE statement. The entire group of declaratives is preceded by DECLARATIVES and followed by END DECLARATIVES in area A.

The three types of declaratives are:
1. Exception (when error occurs during file handling).
2. Debugging (to debug lines with 'D' coded in w-s section).
3. Label (for EOF or beginning...) declaratives.

Question 10: Difference between PIC 9.99 and 9v99

What is the difference between PIC 9.99 and 9v99?

A: PIC 9.99 is a four-position field that actually contains a decimal point while PIC 9v99 is three-position numeric field with implied or assumed decimal position.

Question 11: Use of the Common Attribute

When is the COMMON attribute used?

A: COMMON attribute is used with nested COBOL programs. If it is not specified, other nested programs cannot access the program.

PROGRAM-ID Pgmname is COMMON PROGRAM.

Question 12: Picture 9v99

What is Picture 9v99 Indicates?

A: Picture 9v99 is a three position numeric field with an implied or assumed decimal point after the first position. The v means an implied decimal point.

Question 13: Local-Storage Section

What is a LOCAL-STORAGE SECTION?

A: Local-Storage is allocated each time the program is called and is de-allocated when the program returns in an EXIT PROGRAM, GOBACK, or STOP RUN. Any data items with a VALUE clause are initialized to the appropriate value each time the program is called. The value in the data items is lost when the program returns. It is defined in the DATA DIVISION after WORKING-STORAGE SECTION.

Question 14: Passing by Reference

What does passing BY REFERENCE mean?

A: When the data is passed between programs, the subprogram refers to and processes the data items in the calling program's storage, rather than working on a copy of the data.

When CALL... BY REFERENCE identifier, in this case the caller and the called share the same memory.

Question 15: Passing by Content

What does passing BY CONTENT mean?

A: The calling program passes only the contents of the literal, or identifier. With a CALL . . . BY CONTENT, the called program cannot change the value of the literal or identifier in the calling program, even if it modifies the variable in which it receives the literal or identifier.

Question 16: Guidelines in Writing a Structured COBOL Program

What guidelines should be followed to write a structured COBOL program?

A: You need to use the following guidelines:

1. Use EVALUATE stmt for constructing cases.

2. Use scope terminators for nesting.

3. Use in-line Perform stmt for writing "do" constructions.

4. Use Test Before and Test After in the Perform stmt for writing do-While constructions.

Question 17: Data Types in COBOL

What are the different data types available in COBOL?

A: Alpha-numeric (X), alphabetic (A) and numeric (9).

Question 18: Resolving SOC-7 Error

What do you do to resolve SOC-7 error?

A: You need to correct the offending data. The reason for SOC7 is an un-initialized numeric item. Examine that possibility first. Many installations provide you a dump for run time amends (it can be generated also by calling some subroutines or OS services thru assembly language). These dumps provide the offset of the last instruction at which amend occurred. Examine the compilation output XREF listing to get the verb and the line number of the source code at this offset. Then you can look at the source code to find the bug. To get capture the runtime dumps, you will have to define some datasets (SYSABOUT etc) in the JCL. If none of these are helpful, use judgment and DISPLAY to localize the source of error. You may even use batch program debugging tools.

Question 19: Structures of COBOL Subroutine

How do you define the structure of a COBOL subroutine?

A: The PROCEDURE DIVISION header must have using a phrase if the data needs to be passed to the program. The operands of the USING phrase must be defined in the LINKAGE SECTION as 01-level or 77-level entries. No VALUE clause is allowed unless the data defined is a condition name.

If the program needs to be returned to the CALLER, use EXIT PROGRAM statement at the end of the program. GOBACK is non-standard but can be an alternative.

Question 20: Difference of Next Sentence and Continue

What is the difference between Next Sentence and Continue?

A: Next Sentence gives control to the verb following the next period. While a Continue gives control to the next verb after the explicit scope terminator. This is not one of COBOL II's finer implementations.

It is safer to use Continue rather than Next Sentence in COBOL II. Continue is like a null statement and does nothing, while the Next Sentence transfers control to the next sentence (!!) A sentence is terminated by a period.

You can check it out by writing the following code example. If sentence followed by 3 display statements:

If 1 > 0 then next sentence end if display "line 1" display "line 2" Display "line 3"

Note: There is a dot (.) only at the end of the last 2 statements, see the effect by replacing Next Sentence with Continue ***

Question 21: Structured COBOL and Object Oriented COBOL

What is the difference between Structured COBOL Programming and Object Oriented COBOL programming?

A: Structured programming is a logical way of programming using which you divide the functionality's into modules and code logically. OOP is a natural way of programming in which you identify the objects first then write functions and procedures around the objects. They are two different programming paradigms which are difficult to put in a sentence or two.

Question 22: COMP Preference

Why is it that PIC S (4) is used in spite of COMP-3 which occupies less space?

A: This is because S9 (4) COMP uses only 2 bytes while S9 (4) COMP-3 uses 3 bytes. Having 3 bytes are better than having 2 bytes, that's why COMP is preferred over COMP-3 in this case.

Question 23: Bytes & Digits in S9 (10) COMP

How many number of bytes and digits are involved in S9 (10) COMP?

A: There are 8 bytes (double word) and 10 digits that are involved in S9 (10) COMP. Up to 9(9) comp use in full word and 9(18) comp needed in a double word.

Question 24: Defining Hexadecimal Item in a Value Clause

Which picture clause will you use to define a hexadecimal item in a VALUE clause?

A: You need to use:

```
01 ws-hexitem PIC X (2) value X'020C'.
01 ws-hex redefines PIC S9 (3) comp-3.
```

Question 25: Number of Decimal Digits

How many numbers of decimal digits are possible when the amount of storage allocated for a USAGE COMP item in:

a) Half word?
b) Full word?
c) Double word?

A: You need 2 bytes for half word, 1-4 Digits 4 bytes for full word and for 5-9, 8 bytes for double word for 10-18.

Question 26: Scope Terminator

What is a scope terminator? Can you give examples for this?

A: A Scope Terminator is used to mark the end of a verb.

E.g., EVALUATE, END-EVALUATE; IF, END-IF.

Question 27: Dimensions for a Table

How many dimensions are allowed for a table?

A: There are 7 dimension allowed for a table.

Question 28: Subscripts Allowed for an Occurs Clause

How many subscripts or indexes are allowed for an OCCURS clause?

A: There are 7 subscripts allowed for an Occurs clause.

Question 29: IS NUMERIC Clause

What does the IS NUMERIC clause establish?

A: IS NUMERIC can be used on alphanumeric items, signed numeric & packed decimal items and unsigned numeric & packed decimal items. IS NUMERIC return TRUE if the item only consists of 0-9. However, if the item being tested is a signed item, then it may contain 0-9, + and -.

Question 30: Redefines Clause

Can a Redefines clause be used along with an Occurs clause?

A: Yes, you can use it along with an Occurs clause if the Redefines clause is subordinate to Occurs clause.

Question 31: Difference between OS COBOL and VS COBOL

What is the difference between OS VS COBOL and VS COBOL II?

A: OS/VS COBOL programs can only run in 24 bit addressing mode, VS COBOL II programs can run either in 24 bit or 31 bit addressing modes.

Report writer is supported only in OS/VS Cobol.

USAGE IS POINTER is supported only in VS COBOL II. Reference modification e.g., WS-VAR (1:2) is supported only in VS COBOL II.

EVALUATE is supported only in VS COBOL II.

Scope terminators are supported only in VS COBOL II.

OS/VS Cobol follows ANSI 74 standards while VS COBOL II follows ANSI 85 standards.

Under CICS calls between VS COBOL II programs are supported.

Question 32: Static and Dynamic Linking

What is the difference between Static and Dynamic linking?

A: In static linking, the called subroutine is link-edited into the calling program, while in dynamic linking, the subroutine and the main program will exist as separate load modules. You can choose static/dynamic linking by choosing either the DYNAM or NODYNAM link edit option. Even if you choose NODYNAM, a CALL identifier as opposed to a CALL literal, will translate to a DYNAMIC call. A statically called subroutine will not be in its initial state the next time it is called, unless you explicitly use INITIAL or you do a CANCEL. A dynamically called routine will always be in its initial state.

Question 33: SECTION and PARAGRAPH Difference

What is the difference between performing a SECTION and a PARAGRAPH?

A: A SECTION will cause all the paragraphs that are part of the section to be performed. A PARAGRAPH will cause only that paragraph to be performed.

Question 34: Next and Continue Verbs for File Handling

How do you use Explain NEXT and CONTINUE verbs for file handling?

A: A Continue verb is used for a situation where there is no EOF condition. E.g., the records are to be accessed again and again in a file. Whereas in the next verb, the indexed file is accessed sequentially; therefore, when index clause is accessed sequentially and read, next record command is used.

Question 35: Submit Job from COBOL Programs

How can you submit a job from COBOL programs?

A: Write JCL cards to a dataset with:
//xxxxxxx SYSOUT= (A,INTRDR) where 'A' is output class, and dataset should be opened for output in the program. Define an 80 byte record layout for the file.

Question 36: File Status 39

What is file status 39?

A: Mismatch in LRECL or BLOCKSIZE or RECFM between your COBOL program and the JCL (or the dataset label). You will get file status 39 on an OPEN.

Question 37: SSRANGE and NOSSRANGE

What are SSRANGE and NOSSRANGE?

A: These are compiler options with respect to subscript out of range checking. NOSSRANGE is the default, and if chosen, no run time error will be flagged if your index or subscript goes out of the permissible range.

Question 38: Application of SEARCH

Can a SEARCH be applied to a table which does not have an INDEX defined?

A: No, the table must be indexed.

Question 39: Rules to Perform a Serial Search

What are the different rules applicable to perform a serial SEARCH?

A: The SEARCH can be applied to only a table which has the OCCURS clause and INDEXED BY phrase.

Before using the SEARCH, the index must have some initial value. To search from beginning, set the index value to 1. Use the SEARCH verb without ALL phrases.

Question 40: Open Modes in COBOL

What are different file OPEN modes available in COBOL? In which modes are the files Opened to write?

A: Different Open modes for files are INPUT, OUTPUT, I-O and EXTEND; of which Output and Extend modes are used to write new records into a file.

Question 41: Rules in Performing a Binary Search

What are the different rules applicable to perform a binary SEARCH?

A: The table must be sorted in ascending or descending order before the beginning of the SEARCH. Use OCCURS clause with ASC/DESC KEY IS dataname1 option.

The table must be indexed. You don't need to set the index value. Just use SEARCH ALL verb.

Question 42: How Binary Search Works

How does the binary search work?

A: First, you have to split the table into two halves. The half of desired item that belongs to it should be divided again into two halves and the previous procedure is followed. This will continue until the item is found.

SEARCH ALL is efficient for tables larger than 70 items.

Question 43: Difference between Binary and Sequential Search

What is the difference between a binary search and a sequential search?

What are the pertinent COBOL commands?

A: In a binary search, the table element key values must be in ascending or descending sequence. The table is "halved" to search for equal to, greater than or less than conditions until the element is found.

In a sequential search the table is searched from top to bottom, so the elements don't have to be in a specific sequence.

The binary search is much faster for larger tables, while sequential Search works well with smaller ones.

SEARCH ALL is used for binary searches; SEARCH for sequential.

Question 44: Internal and External Sort

What is the difference between an internal and an external sort?

What are the pros, cons, and internal sort syntax?

How do you define a sort file in JCL that runs the COBOL program?

Which is the default, TEST BEFORE or TEST AFTER for a PERFORM statement?

A: An external sort is not coded as a COBOL program. It is performed through JCL and PGM=SORT. You can use IBM utility SYNCSORT for external sort process. It is understandable without any code reference.

An internal sort can use two different syntaxes:

1. USING, GIVING sorts are comparable to external sorts with no extra file processing.

2. INPUT PROCEDURE, OUTPUT PROCEDURE sorts allows data manipulation before and/or after the sort.

Syntax:

SORT file-1 ON ASCENDING/DESCENDING KEY...
USING file-2 GIVING file-3.
USING can be substituted by INPUT PROCEDURE IS para-1 THRU para-2
GIVING can be substituted by OUTPUT PROCEDURE IS para-1 THRU para-2.

File-1 is the sort work file and must be described using SD entry in FILE SECTION.

File-2 is the input file for the SORT and must be described using an FD entry in FILE SECTION and SELECT clause in FILE CONTROL.

File-3 is the out file from the SORT and must be described using an FD entry in FILE SECTION and SELECT clause in FILE CONTROL.

File-1, file-2, and file-3 should not be opened explicitly.

INPUT PROCEDURE is executed before the sort and records must be released to the sort work file from the input procedure.

OUTPUT PROCEDURE is executed after all records have been sorted.

Records from the sort work file must be returned one at a time to the output procedure.

Use the SORTWK01, SORTWK02, dd names in the step. Number of sort datasets depends on the volume of data being sorted, but a minimum of 3 is required. 45.

TEST BEFORE: by default the condition is checked before executing the instructions under Perform.

Question 45: Rewrite and Delete in ESDS File

Can you rewrite and delete a record in an ESDS file?

A: You can rewrite a record in an ESDS file but you cannot delete.

Just make sure the length is the same when rewriting a record.

Question 46: Perform Test Before and After

What is the difference between Perform with test after and Perform with test before?

A: If TEST BEFORE is specified, the condition is tested at the beginning of each repeated execution of the specified PERFORM range.

If TEST AFTER is specified, the condition is tested at the end of the each repeated execution of the PERFORM range. With TEST AFTER, the range is executed at least once.

Question 47: Coding an In-line Perform

How do you code an in-line PERFORM?

A: You can code an in-line Perform by:
PERFORM ... ... END-PERFORM.

Question 48: WHEN Clause Significance

Is the order of the WHEN Clauses significant in an Evaluate Statement?

A: Yes. Evaluation of the WHEN clauses proceeds from top to bottom and their sequence can determine results.

Question 49: INITIALIZE Default Values

What is the default value(s) for an Initialize and what keyword allows for an override of the default?

A: Initialize sets spaces to alphabetic and alphanumeric fields. Initialize sets zeroes to numeric fields. Filler occurs depending on an item that is left untouched. The replacing option can be used to override these defaults.

Question 50: Set to True

What is set to true all about?

A: In COBOL II, the 88 levels can be set rather than moving their associated values to the related data item.

Web note: This change is not one of COBOL II's better specifications.

Question 51: Length in COBOL II

What is Length in COBOL II?

A: Length acts like a special register to tell the length of a group or an elementary item.

Question 52: Delimiter Function in String

What is the function of a delimiter in String?

A: A delimiter in String causes a sending field to be ended and another to be started.

Question 53: Delimiter in Unstring

What is the function of a delimiter in Unstring?

A: A delimiter when encountered in the sending field causes the current receiving field to be switched to the next one indicated.

Question 54: Number of Characters in a Null-terminated String

How will you count the number of characters in a null-terminated string?

A: You can count the number of characters by:

```
MOVE 0 TO char-count
INSPECT null-terminated-string TALLYING char-count FOR
CHARACTERS BEFORE X"00"
```

Question 55: Move Non-null Characters from a Null-terminated String

Which statement will you use to move non-null characters from a null-terminated String?

A: Unstring null-terminated-string delimited by X"00" into the target-area.

COUNT IN char-count.

There are other methods such as:

1. Using PERFORM
2. Using SEARCH
3. Using INSPECT and MOVE, etc.

Question 56: DATA-2 and COUNTER Results

77 COUNTR PIC 9 VALUE ZERO.
01 DATA-2 PIC X (11). . .
INSPECT DATA-2
TALLYING COUNTR FOR LEADING "0"
REPLACING FIRST "A" BY "2" AFTER INITIAL "C"

If DATA-2 is 0000ALABAMA, what will DATA-2 and COUNTER be after the execution of INSPECT verb?

A: The Counter=4. Data-2 will not change as the Initial 'C' is not found.

Question 57: DATA-4 Before and After Conversion

01 DATA-4 PIC X (11).
:::
INSPECT DATA-4 CONVERTING
"abcdefghijklmnopqrstuvwxyz" TO
"ABCDEFGHIJKLMNOPQRSTUVWXYZ"
AFTER INITIAL "/" BEFORE INITIAL"?"

What will the contents of DATA-4 be after the conversion statement is performed, if before conversion?

a) DATA-4 = a/five/? six
b) DATA-4 = r/Rexx/RRRr
c) DATA-4 = zfour?inspe

A: It will be as follows:

a) a/FIVE/?six
b) r/REXX/RRRR
c) zfour? inspe (no change at all)

Question 58: ON SIZE ERROR

What kind of error is trapped by ON SIZE ERROR option?

A: It's the Fixed-point overflow. Zero raised to the zero power.

Division by 0. Zero raised to a negative number.
A negative number raised to a fractional power.

Question 59: Replacing Option of a Copy Statement

What is the point of the REPLACING option of a copy statement?

A: Replacing allows the same copy to be used more than once in the same code by changing the replace value.

COPY xxx REPLACING BY.

Question 60: Scope Terminator Mandatory

When is a scope terminator mandatory?

A: Scope terminators are mandatory for in-line Performs and Evaluate statements. For readability, it is recommended that coding practice always make scope terminators explicit.

Question 61: Set a Return Code

How do you set a return code to the JCL from a COBOL program?

A: Move a value to RETURN-CODE register. RETURN-CODE should not be declared in your program.

Question 62: Define Different Record Descriptions

How will you define your record descriptions in the File Section if you want to use three different record descriptions for the same file?

A: FD filename:

DATA RECORDS ARE rd01, rd02, rd03.
01 rd01 PIC X (n).
01 rd02 PIC X (n).
01 rd03 PIC X (n).

Question 63: Open a File in the EXTEND Mode

When will you open a file in the EXTEND mode?

A: When an existing file should be appended by adding new records at its end. EXTEND mode opens the file for output, but the file is positioned following the last record on the existing file.

Question 64: Function of Close with Lock

What does a Close with Lock statement do?

A: The statement closes an opened file and it prevents the file from being opened by the same program.

Question 65: Mode Required when REWRITE

Which mode of opening is required when REWRITE is used?

A: It is the I-O mode.

Question 66: I-O Mode

Why is it necessary that the file be opened in I-O mode for REWRITE?

A: Before the REWRITE is performed, the record must be read from the file; hence, REWRITE includes an input operation and an output operation. Therefore, the file must be opened in I-O mode.

Question 67: FILE STATUS = 10

Which clause can be used instead of checking for FILE STATUS = 10?

A: FILE STATUS 10 is the end of file condition; hence, AT END clause can be used.

Question 68: SORT Format

What is the format of a simple SORT verb? What kind of files can be sorted using SORT?

A: The format is: "SORT workfile ON ASC/DESC KEY key1, ASC/DESC KEY key2... USING input file GIVING output file."

Only sequential files can be sorted in this way.

Question 69: Rules of SORT

What are the different rules of SORT that needs to be considered?

A: The input and output files must remain closed because SORT opens them and closes during the operation. The work file must have a SELECT clause. The work file must have sort description SD entry in the FILE SECTION. Input and Output files must have FD entries.

Question 70: Input and Output Procedure

What are INPUT PROCEDURE and OUTPUT PROCEDURE?

A: It is necessary that the records must be edited before or after the sorting. In such cases:

SORT workfile ASC/DESC KEY key1...

INPUT PROCEDURE is ipproc

OUTPUT PROCEDURE is outproc;

In the INPUT PROCEDURE, the input file is opened, records are read and edited and then are released to the sorting operation. Finally, the file is closed.

RELEASE sortrecname FROM inp-rec.

In the OUTPUT PROCEDURE, output file is opened, the sorted record is returned to the Output record area and then the record is written. Finally, the file is closed. RETURN workfile RECORD into out-rec.

Question 71: Simple MERGE Verb Format

What is the format of a simple MERGE verb? Can INPUT PROCEDURE and OUTPUT PROCEDURE be specified for MERGE verb?

A: The MERGE work files are ON ASC/DESC KEY key1...

USING inputfile1, inputfile2... GIVING output file.

INPUT PROCEDURE cannot be specified. Only OUTPUT PROCEDURE can be specified.

Question 72: Start Indexed File

How will you position an indexed file at a specific point so that the subsequent sequential operations on the file can start from this point?

A: Use START:

START filename KEY IS EQ/GT/LT... Data name INVALID KEY.

Question 73: Access Mode of START

What are the access mode requirements of START statement?

A: Access mode must be SEQUENTIAL or DYNAMIC.

Question 74: Opening Mode of START

What are the opening mode requirements of START statement?

A: Files must be opened in the INPUT or I-O mode.

Question 75: Use of Linkage Section

What is the LINKAGE SECTION used for?

A: The linkage section is used to pass data from one program to another program or to pass data from a PROC to a program. It is part of a called program that "links" or maps to data items in the calling program's working storage. It is the part of the called program where these share items are defined.

Question 76: Subscript or Index

Which is preferable if you were passing a table via linkage, a subscript or an index?

A: It's not possible to pass an index via linkage. The index is not part of the calling programs working storage. Indexing uses binary displacement. Subscripts use the value of the occurrence.

Question 77: Difference between Subscript and Index

What is the difference between a subscript and an index in a table definition?

A: Subscript is a working storage data definition item, typically a PIC (999) where a value must be moved to the subscript and then increment or decrement it by ADD TO and SUBTRACT FROM statements.

An index is a register item that exists outside the program's working storage. You SET an index to a value and SET it UP BY value and DOWN BY value.

Subscript refers to the array occurrence while index is the displacement (in no of bytes) from the beginning of the array.

An index can only be modified using PERFORM, SEARCH & SET. You need to have index for a table in order to use SEARCH, SEARCH ALL COBOL statements.

Question 78: In-line Perform

What is an In-line PERFORM? When would you use it?

A: The PERFORM and END-PERFORM statements bracket all COBOL II statements between them. The COBOL equivalent is to PERFORM or PERFORM THRU a paragraph. In line Performs work as long as there are no internal GO TOs, not even to an exit. The in line PERFORM for readability should not exceed a page length—often it will reference other PERFORM paragraphs. The body of the Perform will not be used in other paragraphs. If the body of the Perform is a generic type of code (used from various other places in the program), it would be better to put the code in a separate para and use PERFORM paraname rather than in-line perform.

Question 79: Use of Evaluate Statement

What is the use of EVALUATE statement? How do you come out of an EVALUATE statement?

A: Evaluate is like a case statement and can be used to replace nested Ifs. The difference between EVALUATE and case is that no "break" is required for EVALUATE. When control comes out of the EVALUATE as soon as one match is made, there is no need of any extra code. EVALUATE can be used in place of the nested IF THEN ELSE statements.

Question 80: Different Forms of Evaluate Statement

What are the different forms of EVALUATE statement?

A: They are as follows:

```
 EVALUATE SQLCODE ALSO FILE-STATUS
WHEN A=B AND C=D WHEN 100 ALSO '00'
Imperative stmt imperative stmt
WHEN (D+X)/Y = 4 WHEN -305 ALSO '32'
Imperative stmt imperative stmt
WHEN OTHER WHEN OTHER
Imperative stmt imperative stmt
END-EVALUATE
EVALUATE SQLCODE ALSO A=B EVALUATE SQLCODE ALSO
TRUE
WHEN 100 ALSO TRUE WHEN 100 ALSO A=B
Imperative stmt imperative stmt
WHEN -305 ALSO FALSE WHEN -305 ALSO (A/C=4)
Imperative stmt imperative stmt
END-EVALUATE
```

Question 81: INSPECT in CICS COBOL Program

Can you use the INSPECT (with TALLYING option) COBOL verb in a CICS COBOL program?

A: Yes, under COBOL II environment, but not OS/VS COBOL.

Question 82: Explicit Scope Terminator

What is an explicit scope terminator?

A: A scope terminator brackets its preceding verb, e.g., IF... END-IF, so that all statements between the verb and its scope terminator are grouped together. Other common COBOL II verbs are READ, PERFORM, and EVALUATE, SEARCH and STRING.

Question 83: Significance of "Above and Below the Line"

What is the significance of "above the line" and "below the line"?

A: Before IBM introduced MVS/XA architecture in the 1980's a program's virtual storage was limited to 16 Megs. Programs compiled with a 24-bit mode can only address 16 MB of space, as though they were kept under an imaginary storage line. With COBOL II a program compiled with a 31 bit mode can be "above" the 16 Mb line. (This below the line/above the line imagery confuses most mainframe programmers, who tend to be a literal minded group.)

COMP:
Comp is used for Binary Representation.
It allows only S and 9.
s9 (01) to s9 (04) it takes 2 bytes memory;
s9 (05) to s9 (09) it takes 4 bytes memory;
s9 (10) to s9 (18) it takes 8 bytes memory;

COMP-3:
Comp-3 is used for Packed Decimal values.
It allows S, 9, V.
Mostly it is useful for Decimal Calculation Values.
It takes (n/2)+1 Bytes Memory.

Question 84: Removed from COBOL

What was removed from COBOL in the COBOL II implementation?

A: Here is a partial list:

REMARKS, NOMINAL KEY, PAGE-COUNTER, CURRENT-DAY, TIME-OF-DAY, STATE, FLOW, COUNT, EXAMINE, EXHIBIT, READY TRACE and RESET TRACE.

Question 85: Call Compare

How do you compare call by context to other calls?

A: The parameters passed in a call by context are protected from modification by the called program. In a normal call they are able to be modified.

Question 86: Difference between Comp and Comp-3

What is the difference between comp and comp-3 usage?

Comp is a binary usage, while comp-3 indicates packed decimal. The other common usages are binary and display. Display is the default. Comp is defined as the fastest/preferred numeric data type for the machine it runs on. IBM Mainframes are typically binary and AS400's are packed. I understand the possible causes for SoC1 & SoC4 abends, but what are they really?

A: A SoC1 occurs if the CPU attempts to execute binary code that isn't a valid machine instruction; e.g., if you attempt to execute data. A SoC4 is a memory protection violation. This occurs if a program attempts to access storage beyond the areas assigned to it.

Question 87: Edit Data Items

What happens when we move a comp-3 field to an edited (say z (9).zz-) version?

A: The editing characters are to be used with data items with usage clause as display, which is the default. When you try displaying a data item with usage as computational it does not give the desired display format because the data item is stored as packed decimal. So if you want this particular data item to be edited, you have to move it into a data item whose usage is display and then have that particular data item edited in the format desired.

Question 88: SOC Causes

What are the causes for SoC1, SoC4, SoC5, SoC7, SoCB amends?

A: SoC1 may be due to:
1. Missing or misspelled DD name.
2. Read/Write to unopened dataset.
3. Read to dataset opened output.
4. Write to dataset opened input.
5. Called subprogram not found.

SoC4 may be due to:
1. Missing Select statement (during compile).
2. Bad Subscript/index.
3. Protection Exception.
4. Missing parameters on called subprogram.
5. Read/Write to unopened file.
6. Move data from/to unopened file.

SoC5 May be due to:
1. Bad Subscript/index.
2. Close an unopened dataset.
3. Bad exit from a perform.
4. Access to I/O area (FD) before read.

SoC7 may be due to:
1. Numeric operation on non-numeric data.
2. Un-initialize working-storage.
3. Coding past the maximum allowed sub script.

SoCB may be due to Division by Zero.

Question 89: Use GO BACK Instead of STOP RUN

What will happen if you code GO BACK instead of STOP RUN in a stand-alone COBOL program, i.e., a program which is not calling any other program?

A: Both give the same results when a program is not calling any other program.

Question 90: Difference of External and Global Variables

What is the difference between an External and a Global Variables?

A: Global variables are accessible only to the batch program whereas external variables can be referenced from any batch program residing in the same system library.

Question 91: Report-Item

What is a Report-Item?

A: A Report-Item is a field to be printed that contains EDIT SYMBOLS.

Question 92: Check for Breaks

You are writing a report program with 4 levels of totals: city, state, region and country. The codes being used can be the same over the different levels, meaning a city code of 01 can be in any number of states, and the same applies to state and region code show.

Do you do your checking for breaks and how do you add to each level?

A: Always compare on the highest-level first because if you have a break at a highest level, each level beneath it must also break. Add to the lowest level for each rec but add to the higher level only on break.

Question 93: PSB and ACB

What are PSB and ACB?

A: PSB: Program specification block. Information about how a specific program is to be accessed on one or more IMS DB. It consists of PCB (Program Communication Block). Information to which segment in DB can be accessed, what the program is allowed to do with those segment and how the DB is to be accessed.

ACB: Access Control Blocks are generated by IMS as an expansion of information contained in the PSB in order to speed up the access to the applicable DBDs.

Question 94: Linear Data Set

What's a LDS (Linear Data Set) and what's it used for?

A: LDS is a VSAM dataset in name only. It has unstructured 4k (4096 bytes) fixed size CIs which do not contain control fields and therefore from VSAM's standpoint they do not contain any logical records. There is no free space, and no access from COBOL. It can be accessed by DB2 and IMS fast path datasets. LDS is essentially a table of data maintained on disk. The 'table entries' must be created via a user program and can only be logically accessed via a user program. When passed, the entire LDS must be mapped into storage, and then data is accessed via base and displacement type processing.

Question 95: Importance of Global Clause

What is the importance of GLOBAL Clause according to new standards of COBOL?

A: The importance of Global Clause is that when any data name, file-name, Record-name, condition name or Index defined in an Including Program can be referenced directly or indirectly in an included program. It is provided that the said name has been declared to be a global name by GLOBAL Format of Global Clause is01 data-1 PIC 9(5) IS GLOBAL.

Question 96: Purpose of Pointer Phrase in String Command

What is the purpose of POINTER phrase in STRING COMMAND?

A: The purpose of POINTER phrase is to specify the leftmost position within receiving field where the first transferred character will be stored.

Question 97: Get Current Date with Century

How do we get current date from system with century?

A: By using intrinsic function, FUNCTION CURRENT-DATE.

Question 98: The Difference between Search and Search All

What is the difference between search and search all in the table handling?

A: Search is a linear search and search all is a binary search.

Question 99: Length of Field using COMP-3

What is the maximum length of a field you can define using COMP-3?

A: The maximum length is 10 Bytes (S9 (18) COMP-3).

Question 100: Difference between COBOL and COBOL II

What are the differences between COBOL and COBOL II?

A: The following is not present in COBOL:

The END Delimiter --> END-READ
                      END-PERFORM
                      END-IF
The INITIALIZE VERB
The NESTED DEPENDING ON IN THE OCCURS CLAUSE
NOT AT END IN THE READ STATEMENT
THE ADDRESS OF SPECIAL REGISTER

Question 101: Explicit Scope Terminator

What is an explicit scope terminator?

A: Terminators like END-PERFORM END-EVALUATE are called explicit scope terminators available in COBOL 85.

Question 102: Linkage Section

What is the linkage section?

A: This section allows the user to pass values to the program thru JCL.Eg:Dates for processing the data in the program.

To pull in parameters from the JCL you would use the accept verb.

Question 103: The Difference between Subscript and Index

What is the difference between a subscript and an index in a table definition?

A: A subscript tells the occurrence of a table. Index tells the displacement of the table. Subscript is a working storage variable. Index is not a working storage variable. Never use both index and subscript combined.

Question 104: AMODE (24), AMODE (31), RMODE (24) and RMODE (ANY)

What is AMODE (24), AMODE (31), RMODE (24) and RMODE (ANY)? (Applicable to only MVS/ESA).

A: These are compile/link edit options:

AMODE - Addressing mode. RMODE - Residency mode.
AMODE (24) - 24 bit addressing.
AMODE (31) - 31 bit addressing.
AMODE (ANY) - Either 24 bit or 31 bit addressing depending on RMODE.
RMODE (24) - Resides in virtual storage below 16 Meg line.

Use these for 31 bit programs that call 24 bit programs. (OS/VS Cobol programs use 24 bit addresses only). RMODE (ANY) can reside above or below 16 Meg line.

Question 105: SET TO TRUE

What is SET TO TRUE all about, anyway?

A: The set to true is done for 88 level variables to set that flag.

For example:

```
05 ws-change-flag   pic x (1).
      88 ws-chg      value 'Y'
      88 ws-no-chg   value 'N'
```

When set ws-chg to true is done then ws-change-flag contains value Y. It is the same as moving Y to ws-change-flag.

If the statement is set ws-no-chg to true then ws-change-flag contains value N. It is the same as moving N to ws-change-flag.

At one point of time only one flag can be set.

Question 106: REPLACING Option

What is the point of the REPLACING option of a copy statement?

A: It is as follows:

```
COPY AR00RB REPLACING ==:AR00:== BY ==AMBS==.
AR00RB COPY BOOK AS FOLLOWS AS (I am copying only few
lines of code)
01:AR00: RB-WORK-AREA
03:AR00: RB-IO-REQUEST PIC S9 (04)     BINARY
                         VALUE ZERO
88:AR00: RB-OPEN-INPUT          VALUE +01.
88:AR00: RB-OPEN-OUTPUT         VALUE +02.
88:AR00: RB-OPEN-IO             VALUE +03.
88:AR00: RB-OPEN-INPUT-DYN      VALUE +04.
88:AR00: RB-OPEN-OUTPUT-DYN     VALUE +05.
88:AR00: RB-OPEN-IO-DYN         VALUE +06.
88:AR00: RB-OPEN-INPUT-RDM      VALUE +07.
88:AR00: RB-OPEN-OUTPUT-RDM     VALUE +08.
88:AR00: RB-OPEN-IO-RDM         VALUE +09.
88:AR00: RB-START-GTE           VALUE +10.
```

Here that copy statement replace with AMBS in place: AR00:

So this routine is useful for all files to open, read, write, close, delete, etc.

Question 107: Division Names in COBOL Program

What are the names in the divisions in a COBOL program?

A: IDENTIFICATION DIVISION, ENVIRONMENT DIVISION, DATA DIVISION, PROCEDURE DIVISION.

Question 108: Data Types in COBOL

What are the different data types available in COBOL?

A: These are the Alpha-numeric (X), alphabetic (A), and numeric (9).

Question 109: Initialize Verb Functions

What does the INITIALIZE verb do?

A: The initialize verb does the following:

Alphabetic, Alphanumeric fields, & alphanumeric edited items are set to SPACES.

The Numeric and Numeric edited items are used to set to ZERO.

The FILLER OCCURS DEPENDING ON items left untouched.

Question 110: Use of 77 Levels

What are 77 levels used for?

A: It is an elementary level item. It cannot be subdivisions of other items (cannot be qualified), nor can they be subdivided themselves.

Question 111: Use of 88 Levels

What are 88 levels used for?

A: They are used for condition names.

Question 112: Use of 66 Levels

What are 66 levels used for?

A: They are used for RENAMES clause.

Question 113: IS NUMERIC Clause

What does the IS NUMERIC clause establish?

A: The IS NUMERIC can be used on alphanumeric items, signed numeric & packed decimal items and unsigned numeric & packed decimal items. IS NUMERIC return TRUE if the item only consists of 0-9. However, if the item being tested is a signed item, then it may contain 0-9, + and - .

Question 114: Creating COBOL Program

What are the steps needed when creating a COBOL program executable?

A: The things to be used are:

DB2 precompiler (if embedded SQL used), CICS translator (if CICS pgm), COBOL compiler, and Link editor.

If using a DB2 program, create plan by binding the DBRMs.

Question 115: OCCURS Clause

Can the OCCURS clause be at the 01 level?

A: No, it cannot be.

Question 116: Difference between Index and Subscript

What is the difference between index and subscript?

A: Subscript refers to the array occurrence while index is the displacement (in no of bytes) from the beginning of the array. An index can only be modified using PERFORM, SEARCH & SET.

Need to have index for a table in order to use SEARCH, SEARCH ALL.

Question 117: Difference between Search and Search All

What is the difference between SEARCH and SEARCH ALL?

A: The differences are as follows:

SEARCH: is a serial search.

SEARCH ALL: is a binary search & the table must be sorted (ASCENDING/DESCENDING KEY clause to be used & data loaded in this order) before using SEARCH ALL.

Question 118: Sorting Order for SEARCH ALL

What should be the sorting order for SEARCH ALL?

A: It can be either ASCENDING or DESCENDING. ASCENDING is default. If you want the search to be done on an array sorted in descending order, then while defining the array, you should give DESCENDING KEY clause. (You must load the table in the specified order).

Question 119: Binary Search

What is a binary search?

A: It is a search on a sorted array. Compare the item to be searched with the item at the center. If it matches, fine. If not, repeat the process with the left half or the right half depending on where the item lies.

Question 120: Program Does Not Amend

My program has an array defined to have 10 items. Due to a bug, I find that even if the program accesses the 11th item in this array, the program does not amend. What is wrong with it?

A: You must use compiler option SSRANGE if you want array bounds checking. Default is NOSSRANGE.

Question 121: Sorting COBOL Program

How do you sort in a COBOL program?
Can you give sort file definition, sort statement syntax and meaning?

A: Here's the syntax:

SORT file-1 ON ASCENDING/DESCENDING KEY....
USING file-2
GIVING file-3.
USING can be substituted by INPUT PROCEDURE IS
para-1 THRU para-2

GIVING can be substituted by OUTPUT PROCEDURE IS para-1 THRU para-2.

File-1 is the sort work file and must be described using SD entry in FILE SECTION.

File-2 is the input file for the SORT and must be described using an FD entry in FILE SECTION and SELECT clause in FILE CONTROL.

File-3 is the output file from the SORT and must be described using an FD entry in FILE SECTION and SELECT clause in FILE CONTROL.

File-1, file-2, and file-3 should not be opened explicitly.

INPUT PROCEDURE is executed before the sort and records must be released to the sort work file from the input procedure.

OUTPUT PROCEDURE is executed after all records have been sorted. Records from the sort work file must be returned one at a time to the output procedure.

Question 122: Defining a File in JCL in COBOL Program

How do you define a sort file in JCL that runs the COBOL program?

A: Use the SORTWK01, SORTWK02, dd names in the step. The number of sort datasets depends on the volume of data being sorted, but a minimum of 3 is required.

Question 123: Difference between Performing Section and Paragraph

What is the difference between performing a SECTION and a PARAGRAPH?

A: Performing a SECTION will cause all the paragraphs that are part of the section, to be performed while performing a PARAGRAPH will cause only that paragraph to be performed.

Question 124: Use of Evaluate Statement

What is the use of EVALUATE statement?

A: Evaluate is like a case statement and can be used to replace nested Ifs. The difference between EVALUATE and case is that no 'break' is required for EVALUATE, i.e., control comes out of the EVALUATE as soon as one match is made.

Question 125: Different Forms of Evaluate Statement

What are the different forms of EVALUATE statement?

A: They are as follows:

```
EVALUATE SQLCODE ALSO FILE-STATUS
WHEN A=B AND C=D WHEN 100 ALSO '00'
Imperative stmt imperative stmt
WHEN (D+X)/Y = 4 WHEN -305 ALSO '32'
Imperative stmt imperative stmt
WHEN OTHER WHEN OTHER
Imperative stmt imperative stmt
END-EVALUATE
EVALUATE SQLCODE ALSO A=B EVALUATE SQLCODE ALSO
TRUE
WHEN 100 ALSO TRUE WHEN 100 ALSO A=B
Imperative stmt imperative stmt
WHEN -305 ALSO FALSE WHEN -305 ALSO (A/C=4)
Imperative stmt imperative stmt
END-EVALUATE
```

Question 126: Coming Out of an Evaluate Statement

How do you come out of an EVALUATE statement?

A: After the execution of one of the when clauses, the control is automatically passed on to the next sentence after the EVALUATE statement. There is no need of any extra code.

Question 127: Complex Condition in an EVALUATE Statement

In an EVALUATE statement, can I give a complex condition on a when clause?

A: Yes, you can give a complex condition on a web clause.

Question 128: Define the Structure of a COBOL Subroutine

How to define the structure of a COBOL subroutine?

A: The PROCEDURE DIVISION header must have a USING phrase, if the data needs to be passed to the program. The operands of the USING phrase must be defined in the LINKAGE SECTION as 01-level or 77-level entries. No VALUE clause is allowed unless the data defined is a condition name.

If the program needs to be returned to the CALLER, use EXIT PROGRAM statement at the end of the program. GOBACK is an alternative, but it is nonstandard.

Question 129: Do In-line Performs

How do you do in-line PERFORMS?

A: Use the following Syntax:

PERFORM......
END PERFORM

Question 130: Use of In-line Perform

When would you use in-line perform?

A: When the body of perform will not be used in other paragraphs. If the body of perform is a generic type of code (used from various other places in the program), it would be better to put the code in a separate para and use PERFORM paraname rather than in-line perform.

Question 131: Difference between Continue and Next Sentence

What are the differenced between Continue and Next Sentence?

A: CONTINUE is like a null statement (do nothing), while NEXT SENTENCE transfers control to the next sentence. A sentence is terminated by a period.

Question 132: EXIT

What does EXIT do?

A: It does nothing! If used, it must be the only sentence within a paragraph.

Question 133: Redefining X (100) Field with X (200) Field

Can I redefine an X (100) field with a field of X (200)?

A: Yes you can. "Redefining" just causes both fields to start at the same location. For example:

```
01 WS-TOP PIC X (1)
01 WS-TOP-RED REDEFINES WS-TOP PIC X (2).
If you MOVE '12' to WS-TOP-RED,
DISPLAY WS-TOP will show 1 while
DISPLAY WS-TOP-RED will show 12.
```

Question 134: Redefining X (200) Field with X (100) Field

Can I redefine an X (200) field with a field of X (100)?

A: Yes, you can redefine an X (200) field with a field of X (100).

Question 135: Resolving SOC-7 Error

How can I resolve SOC-7 Error?

A: Basically you need to correct the offending data.

Many times the reason for SOC7 is an un-initialized numeric item. Examine that possibility first.

Many installations provide you a dump for run time amends (it can also be generated by calling some subroutines or OS services thru assembly language). These dumps provide the offset of the last instruction at the amend that occurred. Examine the compilation output XREF listing to get the verb and the line number of the source code at this offset. Then you can look at the source code to find the bug. To get capture the runtime dumps, you will have to define some datasets (SYSABOUT etc) in the JCL.
If none of these are helpful, use judgment and DISPLAY to localize the source of error.

Some installation might have batch program debugging tools. Use them.

Question 136: Storing a Sign in Packed Fields and in Zoned Decimal Fields

How is sign stored in Packed Decimal fields and Zoned Decimal fields?

A: Packed Decimal fields: Sign is stored as a hex value in the last nibble (4 bits) of the storage.

Zoned Decimal fields: As a default, sign is over punched with the numeric value stored in the last bite.

Question 137: Storing a Sign in Comp-3 Field

How is sign stored in a comp-3 field?

A: It is stored in the last nibble. For example if your number is +100, it stores hex 0C in the last byte, hex 1C if your number is 101, hex 2C if your number is 102, hex 1D if the number is -101, hex 2D if the number is -102, etc.

Question 138: LOCAL-STORAGE SECTION

What is LOCAL-STORAGE SECTION?

A: Local-Storage is allocated each time the program is called and is de-allocated when the program returns via an EXIT PROGRAM, GOBACK, or STOP RUN. Any data items with a VALUE clause are initialized to the appropriate value each time the program is called. The value in the data items is lost when the program returns. It is defined in the DATA DIVISION after WORKING-STORAGE SECTION.

Question 139: COMP & COMP-3

What is the difference between COMP & COMP-3?

A: COMP is a binary storage format while COMP-3 is packed decimal format.

Question 140: COMP-1 and COMP-2

What are COMP-1 and COMP-2?

A: COMP-1: Single precision floating point. It uses 4 bytes.

COMP-2: Double precision floating point. It uses 8 bytes.

Question 141: INITIALIZE Verb

What does the INITIALIZE verb do?

A: Alphabetic, Alphanumeric fields, & alphanumeric edited items are set to SPACES. Numeric, Numeric edited items set to ZERO. FILLER, OCCURS DEPENDING ON items left untouched.

Question 142: Bytes for S9 (7) COMP-3 Field

How many bytes do a S9 (7) COMP-3 field occupy?

A: It will take 4 bytes. Sign is stored as hex value in the last nibble.

The general formula is INT $((n/2) + 1))$, where n=7 in this example.

Question 143: Bytes for S9 (7) Sign Trailing Separate Field

How many bytes does a S9 (7) SIGN TRAILING SEPARATE field occupy?

A: It will occupy 8 bytes. There's one extra byte for a sign.

Question 144: Bytes of S9 (8) COMP Field

How many bytes will S9 (8) COMP field occupy?

A: It has 4 bytes.

Question 145: Difference between OS COBOL and VS COBOL II

What are the differences between OS VS COBOL and VS COBOL II?

A: The differences are:

1. OS/VS Cobol programs can only run in 24 bit addressing mode, VS COBOL II programs can run either in 24 bit or 31 bit addressing modes allowing program to address above 16 Meg main storage line.

2. Report writer is supported only in OS/VS Cobol.

3. USAGE IS POINTER is supported only in VS COBOL II.

4. Reference modification, e.g., WS-VAR (1:2) is supported only in VS COBOL II.

5. COBOL II introduces new features (EVALUATE, SET ... TO TRUE, CALL ... BY CONTEXT, etc.).

6. Scope terminators are supported in COBOL II.

7. OS/VS Cobol follows ANSI 74 standards while VS COBOL II follows ANSI 85 standards.

8. Under CICS Calls between VS COBOL II programs are supported.

9. COBOL II supports structured programming by using in-line PERFORMs.

10. COBOL II does not support old features (READY TRACE, REPORT-WRITER, ISAM, etc.).

In non-CICS environment, it is possible. In CICS, this is not possible.

Question 146: Comp Sync

What is COMP SYNC?

A: It causes the item to be aligned on natural boundaries. It can be synchronized left or right. For binary data items, the address resolution is faster if they are located at word boundaries in the memory. For example, on main frame the memory word size is 4 bytes. This means that each word will start from an address divisible by 4. If my first variable is x (3) and next One is s9 (4) comp, then if you do not specify the SYNC clause, S9 (4) COMP will start from byte 3 (assuming that it starts from 0). If you specify SYNC, then the binary data item will start from address 4. You might see some wastage of memory, but the access to this Computational field is faster.

Question 147: Maximum Size of 01 Level in COBOL and COBOL II

What is the maximum size of a 01 level item in COBOL and In COBOL II?

A: The maximum in COBOL II is 16777215.

Question 148: File Format Reference

How do you reference the following file formats from COBOL programs?

A: Use the Fixed Block File: Use ORGANISATION IS SEQUENTIAL. Use RECORDING MODE IS F, BLOCK CONTAINS 0.

Fixed Unblocked Use ORGANISATION IS SEQUENTIAL. Use RECORDING MODE IS F, do not use BLOCK CONTAINS.

Variable Block File: Use ORGANISATION IS SEQUENTIAL. Use RECORDING MODE IS V, BLOCK CONTAINS 0. Do not code the 4 bytes for record length in FD, i.e., JCL rec length will be max rec length in pgm + 4.

Variable Unblocked: Use ORGANISATION IS SEQUENTIAL. Use RECORDING MODE IS V, do not use BLOCK CONTAINS. Do not code 4 bytes for record length in FD i.e. JCL rec length will be max rec length in pgm + 4.

ESDS VSAM file: Use ORGANISATION IS SEQUENTIAL.

KSDS VSAM file: Use ORGANISATION IS INDEXED, RECORD KEY IS, ALTERNATE RECORD KEY IS.

RRDS File: Use ORGANISATION IS RELATIVE, RELATIVE KEY IS.

Printer File: Use ORGANISATION IS SEQUENTIAL. Use RECORDING MODE IS F, BLOCK CONTAINS o. (Use RECFM=FBA in JCL DCB).

Question 149: Files for Open Modes in COBOL

What are the different files for OPEN modes that are available in COBOL?

A: Open for INPUT, OUTPUT, I-O, EXTEND.

Question 150: Storing a Sign in Packed Fields and in Zoned Decimal Fields

How is sign stored in Packed Decimal fields and Zoned Decimal fields?

A: Packed Decimal fields: Sign is stored as a hex value in the last nibble (4 bits) of the storage.

Zoned Decimal fields: As a default, sign is over punched with the numeric value stored in the last bite.

Acknowledgements

All the foregoing was culled from the following websites:

http://www.sourcecodesworld.com/faqs/cobol-faq-part1.asp

http://www.sourcecodesworld.com/faqs/cobol-faq-part2.asp

http://www.sourcecodesworld.com/faqs/cobol-faq-part3.asp

http://www.geekinterview.com/Interview-Questions/Mainframe/COBOL

http://www.geocities.com/srcsinc/COBOLFAQ.html

http://www.sourcecodesworld.com/faqs/cobol-faq-part4.asp

Index